APPLES

A COUNTRY GARDEN COOKBOOK

APPLES

A COUNTRY GARDEN COOKBOOK

By Christopher Idone

Photography by Kathryn Kleinman

CollinsPublishersSanFrancisco

A Division of HarperCollinsPublishers

For Carol, who shared some of my early memories, and
Linda and Barry, good friends, great cooks and best hosts.

First published in USA 1993 by Collins Publishers San Francisco
Copyright © 1993 Collins Publishers San Francisco
Recipes and text copyright © 1993 Christopher Idone
Photographs copyright © 1993 Kathryn Kleinman
Food Stylist: Stephanie Greenleigh
Project Direction, Art Direction and Design: Jennifer Barry
Editor: Meesha Halm
Design and Production Assistant: Cecile Chronister
Production Managers: Jonathan Mills and Lynne Noone
Library of Congress Cataloging-in-Publication Data
Idone, Christopher.
Apples: a country garden cookbook / recipes by Christopher Idone:
photography by Kathryn Kleinman.
p.   cm.
Includes index.
ISBN 0-00-255225-6
1. Cookery (Apples)   I. Title.
TX813.A6136 1993
641.6'41--dc20   CIP 93-7417

Printed in Hong Kong   10 9 8 7 6 5 4 3 2 1

CONTENTS

INTRODUCTION

I think I gave up the Delicious apple long ago on a crisp fall day when a New York street vendor was only charging a nickle an apple. The price was right, but the taste fell far short of the mark. My idea of what an apple should taste like harks back to my childhood when my father's trees produced crisp-skinned, tingling-sweet juicy apples. There were Pippins, Jonathans, Macs and some small old yellow things we could not identify, but boy did they make good applesauce.

My first chore around the house when I was maybe four or five was gathering the apples which had fallen on the ground and filling bushel and peck baskets made of wood. I'd climb the tree to pick from the high branches and toss them to my father or brother. For me it was a game and as much a part of growing up as raking leaves, building gold and red maple-leaf mountains, burying ourselves in them, and having to rake them all over again. It was a time when we could trick or treat without a chaperon and a time when simple games like bobbing for apples kept us giggling and an apple on a string hanging from a doorway was the first time a little boy and girl met face to face.

The apple served another purpose, too. If a tooth was truly loose, my parents had us bite into one and out the tooth would come—the snow-white flesh tinged with spots of blood. It was also a time when we lined our youngest sibling in front of a tree, set an apple on his head, and took turns with a bow and arrow. A sudden scream from my mother put an end to that William Tell fantasy.

But it was the apple picking I remember most about my childhood. The baskets of apples that weren't to be stored or turned into applesauce were packed along with empty bottles and corks into the back of my mother's Ford wagon. My father packed us along, too, and took us to the local cider mill, which belonged to an apple grower who allowed my father to make his own cider. Inside the little barn was what looked like a jerry-rigged wooden machine—a huge wooden tub with a wooden wheel spiked with dowels attached to a jib. A wooden crank turned by hand crushed the apples, and from the spout, autumn's brown juices would flow into a bucket. The barn's pine board walls were damp with apple moisture and the floorboards, slippery. A hill of fermenting skins, stems and seeds was piled in a corner giving off gasses so sharp that the smell made the little kids reel. The pile was destined for the farmer's pigs to get them drunk, no doubt, but also to sweeten them up. We bought pork and hams from that farmer, and oh were those dinners a delicious memory.

Apples were a part of almost every fall and winter meal in my home. We ate applesauce with cream for breakfast, with warm gingerbread when we got home from school, and sandwiched between anise-scented zwiebach that my mother called icebox cake. Stewed apples were served with pork chops at supper time and baked apples were turned into pies, cobblers and turnovers, or put on sticks and dipped into hot sugar syrup colored with red dye Number 2. A crisp, rosy apple always found its way into our lunch pails.

Apples are extremely versatile and nutritious. Although in recent years supermarkets carry a paltry selection, farmers, greengrocers and apple stands along country highways supply us with dozens of varieties from the palest gold to the brightest green, from the faintest pink to a solid ruby. Depending on the variety, apples can taste sweet or tart, juicy or dry, flat or sharp. Their texture varies from silken to mealy and the eating experience, thrilling or just plain dull.

The apple has played a part since the beginning of civilization in religion, mythology, folklore, history and fairy tales. Adam and Eve ate what we traditionally think of as an apple, although it was simply identified as the fruit from the Tree of Knowledge of Good and Evil. Paris gave Aphrodite a golden apple that caused the Trojan War, although it is believed by most historians to have been a quince or an orange. William Tell shot an apple off his son's head and the

Italian composer Rossini turned the incident into music. Snow White's stepmother used an apple to poison her, and Isaac Newton's legendary inspiration was an apple that supposedly fell from the tree under which he was sitting.

When we refer to someone or something as American as apple pie, there is a reason. In colonial times, when the pork barrel ran out, and when the bean pot was emptied, apple pie was more than dessert. It was breakfast, lunch and dinner. "My wife's and my supper half of the year consists of apple pie and milk," wrote Michel Guillaume-Jean de Crevecoeur, a farmer and essayist who lived in New York State in the late 1700s. It wasn't rare for the colonial farmer to have some hundred apple trees in his orchard. A hint of an American nursery is contained in the records of John Endecott of Salem, Massachusetts, who swapped 500 apple trees for 250 acres of land in 1641. By 1730, Robert Prince was developing over 80 varieties on his Long Island farm, and for four successive generations, the Princes would supply the Eastern seaboard with new and old varieties such as the Royal Russet, Leather Coat, American Pippin, American Nonpareil, American Gloriamundi, Cat-Heat, Morgan, Van Winkle and Pearmain—one of the apples first cultivated at the old Plymouth colony. It wasn't until the late 1700s when John Chapman, a.k.a. Johnny Appleseed, started his treck west— not scattering seeds along the wayside as the tale goes—but planting apple saplings. By 1800 he had established a string of nurseries that stretched from the Allegheny River in Pennsylvania to Central Ohio. His favorite apple, the Rambo, can still be bought at some local farm stands today.

The British captain Aemilius Simpson arrived in what is now Washington state in 1824 with a few seeds of an apple he had eaten in London at his farewell party. He later planted them at Fort Vancouver. Although his first tree bore but one apple, its progeny is honored as the ancestor of the Pacific Northwest's apple. Today, Washington is the largest apple producer in the world, followed by New York, Michigan, California and Pennsylvania. The Red Delicious remains the biggest selling crop, with the Golden Delicious and Granny Smith trailing in second and third place.

The esteemed British food writer Jane Grigson tells a story of the apple farmers in Brittany. At the end of the picking season, one last apple is left on the highest branch in the orchard. If it holds to the branch until all the leaves fall, then the orchard will produce a good crop the following year. The apple is indeed a sign of fertility and good luck.

GLOSSARY

Apples have been around for centuries. We know that fossil apple seeds have been found in places as divergent as Asia, prehistoric Swiss lake settlements, and Neolithic sites in England. In 149 B.C., the time of Cato's Rome, there were seven known varieties of apples. Centuries later, in 1628, there were still only seven types grown in the gardens of Louis XIII at Orléans. By the 19th century, however, more than 7,000 varieties of apples had been identified or developed. Of that amount, over 2,500 varieties are available today in the U.S., although only approximately 100 varieties are grown commercially.

Selecting: Apples can be round like a McIntosh or egg-shaped like the Red Delicious. They can vary in size from a one-inch crab apple to a six-inch Cortland. Their flesh may be white as a Rhode Island, yellow as a Golden Delicious, crisp as a Northern Spy, mellow as a Baldwin, sweet as an Idared or tart as a Winesap. Whatever apple you use in cooking, almost all of them have a purpose. When cooking apples, steer towards the green to yellow, firm and tart varieties, and when using them raw, use a less tart red apple. Some apples are tarter than others and may require the addition of sugar when cooking. As a general rule, the greener the apple, the tarter the taste. However, the Golden Delicious when green, is especially sweet and is an exception to this rule. Shiny, bright red apples often belie their tough skins and woody flesh. Apples of red coloring produce a rosy color when cooked with skins on. Yellow or green apples produce a white color.

When calculating how many apples you'll need for a recipe, estimate approximately 3 medium apples per pound. Three pounds yields approximately 9 cups of sliced apples.

Storing: Apples can be kept up to 6 months if properly stored. But there is truth to the old adage "one rotten apple can spoil the barrel." Rotten apples must indeed be discarded or all the others will spoil.

The best apples are bought at farm stands and farmers' markets. They are usually picked the same day or a day or two before being sold. Buy them ahead to ripen a day or two before cooking or eating. To avoid discoloring, toss apple slices with lemon juice or cover them in acidulated water if you are not using them right away. Always dry them well before cooking.

In this glossary, I have listed the apples called for in the recipes along with other suggested apples to look for. Depending on what part of the country you live in, a myriad of apple varieties will be available to you. If you can't find the kind of apple I suggest, feel free to choose a comparable variety. Many varieties are available year round, but are at their best during September to November when newly harvested.

Arkansas Black: Available from December to April. Small, purplish red deepening over nearly black skin; firm, yellow flesh; slightly tart flavor; holds its shape well during cooking.

Baldwin: Available October to April, primarily in the East. Green skin mottled with bright red specks; crisp, yellowish flesh; juicy and mildly tart. Popular in the 1900s, in the North disease almost caused this crop to disappear. Good for eating raw in salads and excellent for baking and cooking.

Cortland: Available September through spring, primarily in the East and Midwest. A McIntosh hybrid; shiny red skin with green highlights; slightly tart, tender white flesh that is slow to oxidize. Great for eating raw in salads.

Criterion: Available October to March nationwide. Yellow skin tinged with red highlights; sweet and juicy white flesh; sometimes called the candy apple; particularly good eaten raw, but fine for baking.

Dolga Crab Apple: Available October to November nationwide. Small, rosy red skins with extremely hard, tart flesh; too sour to eat raw, but delicious when cooked into jams and jellies or baked and served with meats.

Empire: Available September to spring, primarily in the East and upper Midwest. Hybrid of a Red Delicious and McIntosh. Dark red skin, with crisp, juicy white flesh; mildly tart. Excellent for eating raw in salads.

Fuji: Available October to December, in limited supply primarily in California and Washington. Greenish yellow skin with a rosy blush; sweet and juicy; crisp white flesh. Excellent for eating raw in salads but also fine for cooking.

Gala: Available mid-August to December nationwide. Yellow to orange skin with deep orange stripes; firm white flesh; sweet, aromatic and juicy. Delicious for eating raw in salads, but also quite good as a cooking apple for desserts and applesauce.

Golden Delicious: Available year-round nationwide, although harvested in October. Bright yellow to golden skin; bright yellow flesh; sweet, tangy and juicy. Good for eating raw in salads; holds shape well when cooked in tarts and compotes.

Granny Smith: Available year-round nationwide, although harvested in October. Bright green skin; tart and juicy, crisp white flesh. Excellent for all-purpose cooking; holds shape well in sautés, tarts and pies. A large imported crop arrives from New Zealand and Australia in the summer.

Gravenstein: Available Late August to December, primarily on the West Coast. Yellow or green skin with red striations; yellowish flesh; mild, juicy and slightly tart. Good for eating raw in salads as well as for baking and cooking.

Grimes Golden: Available October to January. Medium- to small-sized apple with deep yellow skin and brownish specks; yellow flesh; slightly dry, sweet and spicy. Good for eating raw in salads.

Idared: Available November to April, primarily in the East and Midwest. Bright red skin; white flesh with a juicy, rich, sweet flavor. Good for eating raw in salads and for cooking.

Arkansas Black   Baldwin   Cortland   Criterion

Dolga Crab Apple   Empire   Fuji   Gala   Golden Delicious

Granny Smith   Gravenstein   Grimes Golden   Idared

Jonagold   Jonathan   Lady   McIntosh

Mutsu   Mutsu's Mother   Newtown Pippin   Northern Spy   Red Delicious

Rhode Island Greening   Rome Beauty   Spartan   Winesap

Jonagold: Available September to October nationwide. A cross between a Jonathan and a Golden Delicious; bright crimson blushed over tender, golden yellow skin; rich, sweet, tangy, juicy white flesh; best savored when just picked. Good for eating raw in salads and for cooking.

Jonathan: Available September to June, primarily in the Midwest. Bright red skin over yellow background; highly aromatic white flesh; juicy, slightly tart with good apple flavor. Good for eating raw in salads, yet holds shape well during cooking.

Lady: Available fresh October to May; also available canned. Small, oblong apples with glossy red and yellow skins with red blushing; crisp, slightly acidic, sweet flesh. Good for eating raw in salads and for cooking; lends lovely color to desserts and used widely for decorative purposes.

McIntosh: Available September through March, primarily in the East and Midwest. Bright, deep red skin striped with carmine; whitish flesh; juicy, mild, tart-sweet flavor when ripe. Best eaten raw—does not hold shape well during lengthy cooking.

Mutsu: Available October to February, primarily in the East. An offspring of the Golden Delicious from Japan, often marketed as Crispin. Pale, greenish-yellow skin with some red blush; sweet and spicy; juicy crisp flesh. Excellent for eating raw in salads, but holds shape well during cooking.

Mutsu's Mother: Available October to December. Yellower skin than the Mutsu and speckled with brown. Good for cooking.

Newtown Pippin: Available September to June, primarily on the West Coast. Light green to yellow skin; burnished with yellow; yellow flesh is crisp, sweet and juicy. Good all-purpose apple; great for eating raw in salads, yet maintains its shape and flavor nicely during cooking.

Northern Spy: Available October to March, primarily in the Northeast and Great Lakes regions. Bright red over yellow skin; yellowish flesh; robust flavor, slightly tart and juicy. Great for eating raw in salads and for cooking and baking.

Red Delicious: Available year-round nationwide, although harvested in October. Dark red, tough skin with solid, medium-tart to sweet flesh; sometimes juicy and sometimes mealy; produced more for color than flavor.

Rhode Island Greening: Available October to April, primarily in the East and central U.S. A variant is grown in the West called Northwest Greening. Green or yellowish skin with some red blush; yellowish flesh; very juicy, tender and sweet-tart. Flavor intensifies when cooked, making it an excellent variety for applesauce and baking in pies.

Rome Beauty: Available October to July nationwide. Crimson red mixed with yellow skin; flesh is white to pale green; juicy and slightly tart. Good for cooking and baking.

Spartan: Available October to February, primarily in the Northeast. A McIntosh/Newtown hybrid; dark red skin that resembles a McIntosh; firm, sweet and juicy white flesh. Best for eating raw in salads.

Winesap: Available October through August nationwide. Bright red skin tinged with yellow or green; juicy, spicy and aromatic, slightly tart flesh. Good for eating raw in salads and cooked in pies. Best choice for making cider.

OPENERS

The apple has long been treated as a savory ingredient in cooking. Scandinavians diced them into salads of beet, herring and ham; the Belgians added them to salads of endive and walnuts; the Germans incorporated them into steamed dumplings; and the Pennsylvania Dutch reconstituted dried apples and served them with highly spiced ham called *schnitz* and *knepp*. Central Europe, with its fondness for fruit soups, included them in their lexicon and the maître d'hôtel at The Waldorf Astoria in New York brought American cooking to a more than brief halt with the invention of the Waldorf salad.

Different apples will suit your culinary purposes differently. When cooking apples, steer toward the green to yellow tart varieties that are firm enough to hold their shape. When using apples raw, to complement rich cheeses and add texture and sweetness to salads, you're better off using the red or the less tart varieties. Savory dishes that call for apples are best made with tart, firm apples like Granny Smiths, Rhode Island Greenings, Winesaps or other hard-fleshed, tart apples. A cold apple soup is best made with a sweet apple, whereas Senegalese soup, on the other hand, is best made with a tarter apple to counteract the spice and the sweetness of the chicken, stock and cream.

Apple and Butternut Squash Soup

*The combination of tart green apples and
sweet butternut squash makes a delightfully bright, rich soup.*

3 tablespoons unsalted butter
2 large onions, chopped
2 tablespoons good quality curry powder
1 teaspoon chili powder
5 cups chicken stock,
  homemade or low-sodium canned

1 large butternut squash (approximately 8 cups),
  peeled, seeded and chopped
3 firm, tart apples (such as Granny Smith),
  peeled, cored and diced
Salt and freshly ground black pepper to taste
1/2 cup heavy cream
1 tablespoon chopped fresh parsley or fresh cilantro

In a heavy skillet, melt the butter over medium heat. Add the onions and sauté until translucent, approximately 5 minutes. Add the curry and chili powders and cook for another 5 minutes. Add half the stock and bring to a boil.

Transfer the mixture to a soup kettle, add the squash and apples, and season with salt and pepper. Bring to a boil, reduce the heat and simmer for 45 minutes to 1 hour, or until the squash is tender. Stir occasionally to prevent the vegetables from sticking to the pan.

Strain the soup and reserve the liquid. Place the pulp in the bowl of a food processor and pulse until puréed.

Return the purée, reserved liquid, cream and the remaining chicken stock to a clean soup kettle and bring to a simmer.

Ladle the soup into warm soup bowls and sprinkle with chopped parsley or cilantro.
Serves 10

Note: This soup can be made ahead or frozen without the cream.

Senegalese Soup

*This cold soup made popular at the old "21" Club
is a rich concoction of curry, cream and chicken stock.*

8 cups chicken stock,
   homemade or low-sodium canned
1 carrot, peeled and chopped
3 celery stalks, diced
3 small onions, peeled
3 whole cloves
1 large chicken breast, skin and bone left on

6 tablespoons (3/4 stick) unsalted butter
2 large tart apples (such as Granny Smith),
   peeled, cored and diced
1 tablespoon curry powder or more to taste
1 tablespoon all-purpose flour
1 ounce dry sherry (optional)
Salt and freshly ground white pepper to taste
1 cup heavy cream

In a nonreactive soup kettle, add the stock, carrots, celery, 1 whole onion studded with the cloves and bring to a simmer over medium heat. Add the chicken breast and poach for 15 minutes or until tender. Remove the breast and set aside to cool. When the breast is cool, wrap in plastic wrap and refrigerate. Skim the stock and simmer for another 30 minutes.

Mince the remaining 2 onions. In a medium skillet, melt the butter over medium heat and add the onions and apples. Sauté the mixture until soft, approximately 10 minutes. Stir in the curry powder and cook for another 3 minutes. Add the flour and combine.

Add the sherry and 2 ladles of stock and bring to a simmer. Remove the clove-studded onion from the soup kettle and add the curry mixture to the stock. Season with salt and pepper and simmer for 30 minutes.

Strain the soup into a large bowl. In a food processor, purée the vegetable and apple pulp until smooth and combine with the soup. Add the cream and refrigerate until cold. When ready to serve, skin and bone the chicken breast and cut into small cubes. Divide the chicken among 6 chilled soup bowls and ladle in the cold soup. *Serves 6*

Note: This soup is best made a day ahead.

Cold Apple Soup

A light refresher to start a meal on a sunny fall day.

4 large sweet apples (such as McIntosh, Spartan,
Golden Delicious), peeled, cored and sliced
1 tablespoon lemon juice
1 tablespoon granulated sugar
1/4 teaspoon mace
3 1/2 cups homemade or canned chicken stock
Salt and freshly ground white pepper to taste

1 teaspoon arrowroot
4 thin lemon slices

Crème Fraîche *(prepare ahead of time)*
1 cup lukewarm whipping cream
2 tablespoons buttermilk

1 teaspoon lemon zest

In a nonreactive soup kettle, add the apples and toss with the lemon juice. Add the sugar, mace and stock and bring to a boil. Season with salt and pepper, reduce the heat and simmer for 20 minutes, or until the apples are soft.

Strain the mixture into a bowl and purée the pulp in a food processor or blender.

Mix the arrowroot with a little water and whisk into the soup. Return the mixture to a clean soup kettle and stir over medium heat until glossy and slightly thick, approximately 5 minutes. Remove from the heat and cool slightly. Cover and refrigerate.

Ladle the soup into 4 cold soup plates and place a lemon slice in the center of each with a little crème fraîche sprinkled with lemon zest.

To make the crème fraîche, combine the whipping cream with the buttermilk in a small bowl. Cover and let stand in a warm place for 6 to 24 hours. Stir and refrigerate. Crème fraîche will keep in the refrigerator for up to 1 week. If you are short on time, combine 1/2 cup sour cream with 1/2 cup whipping cream, cover, and let stand for 1 hour. *Serves 4*

Celery and Apple Rémoulade

This classic winter starter is popular
throughout France.

2 large celery roots (celeriac)
1 lemon plus 1 teaspoon lemon juice
1 tart green apple (such as Winesap),
    peeled and cored

Dressing:
2 tablespoons extra virgin olive oil
2 tablespoons Dijon-style mustard
1/3 cup mayonnaise, preferably homemade
3/4 cup sour cream or crème fraîche (see p. 23)
Salt and freshly ground black pepper to taste
1 tablespoon finely chopped fresh parsley

Peel the celery root and rub with half a lemon.
Cut the celery root to fit into the tube of a food
processor and julienne, or slice into julienne on
a mandoline. Place celery root in a bowl.
Reserve 1 teaspoon lemon juice and toss with
the juice of the remaining half lemon.

Slice the apple into julienne on a mandoline
or on the large grating side of a hand grater.
Toss with the celery root and set aside.

Prepare the dressing: In a bowl, whisk the
oil with the mustard. Add the remaining teaspoon of lemon juice and whisk in the mayonnaise and sour cream. Season with salt and
pepper.

Fold the dressing into the celery and apples.
Cover tightly and refrigerate until chilled.

Serve on individual plates and dust with
chopped parsley. *Serves 4 to 6*

Beet, Radicchio and Apple Salad with Roquefort

The fruitiness and refreshing acidity of the
cider-walnut dressing enlivens this colorful salad.

Cider-Walnut Dressing:
2 tablespoons cider vinegar
4 tablespoons walnut oil
2 tablespoons olive oil
1 tablespoon Dijon-style mustard
Salt and freshly ground black pepper to taste

4 medium beets, baked or boiled,
    peeled and cut into julienne
1 large head radicchio,
    trimmed, cored and cut into julienne
1 large endive, trimmed,
    cored and cut widthwise into julienne
1 bunch watercress, trimmed and chopped
2 medium sweet-tart apples
    (such as Northern Spy or Winesap),
    peeled, cored, sliced and cut into julienne
1/4 cup fresh walnuts, shelled
Salt and freshly ground black pepper to taste
4 ounces Roquefort cheese, crumbled

In a large bowl, whisk together the vinegar, oils
and mustard. Season with salt and pepper.

Toss the beets, radicchio, endive, watercress and apples with the cider-walnut dressing.

Toast the walnut meats in a nonstick pan
over high heat for a minute, or until warmed
through. Season with a little salt and pepper.

Divide the salad among 4 chilled salad
plates. Top each salad with some toasted walnuts and Roquefort. *Serves 4*

Beet, Radicchio and Apple Salad with Roquefort

Salmagundi

One of the first composed salads, Salmagundi dates back to 16th century England.

Lemon Vinaigrette:
4 tablespoons lemon juice
Salt and freshly ground black pepper to taste
1/3 cup walnut oil
2 tablespoons canola or vegetable oil

1/4 cup applejack
1/2 cup Sultana (golden) raisins
3/4 pound haricots verts or fresh green beans,
*   cooked al dente, blanched and drained*
1 cup fresh pearl onions, cooked,
*   blanched, and peeled*

2 tart apples (such as Winesap or Granny Smith),
*   peeled, cored and cut into 1/4-inch dice*
1 cup seedless green grapes
1 small head loose leaf lettuce, washed and dried
2 heads bibb lettuce, washed and dried
1 tablespoon capers, washed and drained
3 chicken breasts, poached, boned and skinned,
*   and cut into long julienne*
1/2 sweet red bell pepper, cored, seeded,
*   ribs removed and cut into 1/4-inch dice*
6 quail eggs, hard-boiled, peeled and halved
1 tablespoon fresh snipped chives

In a small bowl, whisk together the lemon juice, salt and pepper. Gradually whisk in the oils and blend. Set aside.

In a saucepan, heat the applejack with 1/4 cup water. Bring to a simmer, add the raisins and set aside to cool.

In a large bowl, toss the haricots verts, onions, apples, grapes, and lettuce with the capers and enough vinaigrette to coat. Divide among 6 serving plates.

Drain the raisins and sprinkle over the salad. Arrange the julienne chicken in the middle of each salad and sprinkle with the diced red bell pepper. Place 2 quail egg halves next to the chicken and sprinkle with chives. *Serves 6*

Grilled Prawns with Winter Fruit Chutney

Though grilling the shrimp on a charcoal fire is the ideal way to prepare this dish,
they can be cooked in a very hot, preheated cast-iron skillet.

24 medium prawns, in their shells
Extra virgin olive oil
Kosher salt and freshly cracked black pepper
1 sweet red bell pepper,
    cored, seeded, ribs removed and cut into strips
1 sweet yellow bell pepper,
    cored, seeded, ribs removed and cut into strips

1 head frisée, washed,
    dried and torn into bite-size pieces
Juice of 1 lemon
Salt and freshly ground black pepper to taste
Vegetable oil for the grill
Winter fruit chutney (see p. 48)

Prepare a charcoal grill.

Wash and pat dry the prawns with paper towels. In a bowl, toss the shrimp with enough olive oil to coat, and add kosher salt and cracked pepper to taste. Set aside for 30 minutes.

In another bowl, toss the peppers with more olive oil and seasonings. Set aside for 30 minutes.

When the coals are a dusty glow, brush the grill with vegetable oil and place the prawns in the middle of the grill and the pepper strips, skin side down, around the shrimp. Cook the shrimp for 3 minutes on each side, or until they are slightly resilient to the touch. When the pepper strips are slightly limp, turn and grill another 3 minutes or until tender.

Toss the frisée with the juice of half a lemon and season with salt and pepper. Divide the frisée among 4 serving plates.

When the shrimp are done, sprinkle with the juice of the remaining half lemon while still on the grill. Divide and arrange the shrimp and peppers over the frisée. Spoon some winter fruit chutney on the side of the plate and serve. Eat shells and all. *Serves 4*

Swiss Chard Salad with Walnuts and Gorgonzola

The marriage of apples and cheese is a classic pairing.
Introduced into a salad, apples add crispness, sweetness and crunch.

2 bunches small-leafed Swiss chard,
*   preferably ruby chard, including the tender ribs*
4 ounces country bacon, cut into 1/4-inch dice
1/4 cup shelled walnuts
1/4 cup walnut oil
1/4 cup canola oil

1 tart apple (such as Gravenstein or Star),
*   peeled, cored and cut into 1/4-inch dice*
Salt and freshly ground black pepper to taste
3 tablespoons raspberry vinegar
4 ounces Gorgonzola, thinly sliced

Wash and dry the Swiss chard, cut into julienne, and set aside.

In a medium skillet, render the bacon over medium heat until golden and drain on paper towel. Drain off most of the fat and lightly toast the walnuts in the pan, making sure they do not burn. Drain on paper towels.

Wipe the skillet clean with a paper towel and add half the walnut oil and half the canola oil over medium-low heat. When the oils are warm, toss in the diced apple and cook until it begins to soften, approximately 4 minutes.

Toss in the chard and season with salt and pepper. Add the vinegar and toss again. Add enough of the remaining oils to coat the chard.

When the chard is wilted, divide the mixture among 4 warm salad plates. Sprinkle each salad with the bacon and walnuts and drizzle the remaining dressing over the salad. Arrange the cheese over each salad. *Serves 4*

Breakfast Apple Omelette

Though the egg has taken a bad rap of late, egg dishes and omelettes are still popular for breakfast or brunch, even if enjoyed only on Sunday.

3 Golden Delicious apples, peeled, cored and chopped
2 tablespoons vanilla sugar or granulated sugar
1 tablespoon Calvados
6 eggs

Pinch of salt
3 tablespoons unsalted butter
Granulated sugar for dusting
Confectioner's sugar (optional)

In a small saucepan, combine the apples and vanilla sugar. If using granulated sugar, add 1/8 teaspoon vanilla extract. Cover and cook over medium heat, shaking the pan from time to time so the apples do not stick. When the apples are soft, remove from the heat and whisk in the Calvados. Cover and set aside.

Preheat the broiler. In a bowl, beat the eggs with salt and 1 tablespoon cold water.

In a 6-inch nonstick pan, melt half the butter over medium heat. Add half the egg mixture, gently whisking the eggs with a fork until the egg mixture coats the bottom and sides of the pan. When the eggs begin to solidify and reach the desired state of doneness, fold in half the apple mixture. Fold the omelette over and continue cooking another minute or so.

Slide the omelette onto a heatproof plate. Dust with a little granulated sugar and glaze under the broiler. Repeat with the remaining ingredients. Sprinkle with confectioner's sugar, if desired. *Makes 2 omelettes*

ACCOMPANIMENTS

The apple is winter's condiment. Of all the fruits, the apple lends itself best to chutneys, butters and sauces. Sautéed, it complements meat, poultry and game birds, and when mixed with horseradish, cream and mustard, it is a delicious accompaniment to rich smoked fish.

The apple on its own also acts as a crisp foil for many foods. The early English cooks tied apples on strings before a hearth, where they roasted them until the apples fell into a bowl of spiced wine placed beneath. After marinating in the warm wine, they were served with their spit-roasted meats.

Apples marry well with sausage and sage for stuffings, and when cooked and puréed with winter root vegetables, they take away the gaseous strength of rutabagas and enliven parsnips. Though straightforward chutneys of apples, raisins and spices can be delicious with anything from pork to meat loaf, the East Indian combination of apples and tamarind will make any curry dish sing.

Apple Fritters

Serve these crunchy crullers with roast pork and pork chops,
braised or boiled beef or sauerbraten.

Batter:
1 egg, beaten
2/3 cup milk
1 tablespoon unsalted butter, melted
1 1/2 cups all-purpose flour
2 teaspoons baking powder
1/8 teaspoon salt

3 tart cooking apples, (such as Granny Smith,
Gravenstein or Winesap), peeled,
cored and cut into 1/3-inch round slices
Juice of 1 lemon
Approximately 2 cups vegetable oil
1 tablespoon granulated sugar

In a large bowl, whisk the egg with the milk and melted butter. Sift in the dry ingredients and blend. Set aside.

Prepare the apples and toss with the lemon juice.

Heat the oil in a deep skillet over high heat until the temperature registers 350 degrees F. on a frying thermometer. Oil should be hot, but not smoking and should bubble immediately when the apples are dropped in it.

Lightly dip the apple slices in the batter. Drop into the oil and fry until golden on both sides, approximately 5 minutes. Remove with a slotted spoon, drain on paper towels and place in a warm oven.

When all the fritters are done, transfer to a serving platter and sprinkle with a little extra lemon juice and sugar. *Serves 4*

Sweet and Sour Red Cabbage

*Sweet and sour red cabbage
can be made a day ahead and reheated. Serve it
with duck, goose or pheasant.*

4 pounds white or red cabbage or a combination
    of both, trimmed, cored and shredded
4 tablespoons (1/2 stick) unsalted butter
1 tablespoon vegetable oil
1 medium onion, finely chopped
2 tart apples (such as Greening or Granny Smith),
    peeled, cored and cut into 1/4-inch dice
1 tablespoon light brown sugar
1/3 cup red wine vinegar
1 cup chicken stock,
    homemade or low-sodium canned
1 teaspoon caraway seeds
Salt and freshly ground black pepper to taste
1/2 cup red currant jelly

In a kettle of lightly salted boiling water, blanch the cabbage for 1 minute. Drain and cool under running water. If using a combination of white and red cabbage, blanch separately. When cool, drain thoroughly and set aside.

In a large nonreactive skillet, heat the butter and oil over medium heat. Add the onions, apples and sugar and sauté for 5 minutes. Stir in the drained cabbage, vinegar and stock, and cook for another 10 minutes, stirring often. Add the carraway seeds, salt, pepper and the currant jelly. Stir, reduce the heat and simmer for another 10 minutes, or until the cabbage is limp. *Serves 5 to 6*

Sauerkraut and Apples

*Serve with grilled pork chops, wursts and sausages,
or to make a quick choucroute—bake with smoked
pork chops or butts, lean bacon and wurst.*

2 pounds sauerkraut, preferably fresh
2 tablespoons goose fat
1 medium onion, coarsely chopped
1 garlic clove minced
1 cup apple cider
1 cup chicken stock,
    homemade or low-sodium canned
3 large tart apples (such as Granny Smith or
    Greening), peeled, cored and coarsely chopped
6 juniper berries, crushed
1 ounce gin (optional)
Salt and freshly ground black pepper to taste

Preheat the oven to 350 degrees F.

Place a colander in a large bowl under cold running water. Add the sauerkraut and wash to remove the brine. Wring dry, pull apart and set aside.

In a large nonreactive skillet, melt the fat over medium heat. Add the onions and garlic and sauté until translucent. Add the sauerkraut, cider, stock, apples and juniper berries and bring to a boil over high heat.

Transfer the mixture to an ovenproof casserole. Add the gin and season with salt and pepper. Cover and bake for 40 minutes.
Serves 6

Pickled Crab Apples

Even today, a dinner or supper at
a Pennsylvania Dutch farm includes condiments
consisting of seven sweets and seven sours.
This recipe is one of them. Serve it with roast pork,
pork chops or braised beef dishes.

Approximately 30 crab apples,
*   with skin and stem intact*
4 cups cider vinegar
4 cups sugar
2 teaspoons pickling spices
3 bay leaves
12 cloves
Six 1-inch pieces cinnamon stick

Place the apples in a heavy, nonreactive kettle. Add the vinegar and enough cold water to cover the apples. Add the remaining ingredients. Bring to a boil over high heat, stirring from time to time. Reduce the heat and simmer for 45 minutes, or until the crab apples are almost tender.

Transfer the apples to sterilized pint jars and divide the spices among the jars. Add the syrup and allow 1/2-inch head space. Seal the jars with canning lids according to manufacturer's directions and process in a boiling water bath for 10 minutes. Cool, tighten lids, and store. Or, cover tightly and keep in the refrigerator up to 3 weeks. *Makes approximately 6 pints*

Applesauce

Yellow apples make a white sauce and
red apples produce a rosy colored sauce. The amount
of sugar used depends on the sweetness of the
apple. When serving as an accompaniment with
meat dishes, a tarter flavor is preferred.

6 to 8 sweet, firm apples
*   (such as Golden Delicious, Idared, Cortland*
*   or combination), peeled, cored, and sliced*
1/3 cup granulated sugar, or to taste
Heavy cream for serving (optional)

Preheat the oven to 350 degrees F.

Place the apples in a 1-quart soufflé dish or casserole and cover with foil. Bake for 30 minutes, or until the apples have puffed up and are tender.

Remove from the oven and crush and whisk the apples until smooth. Whisk in the sugar to taste.

Serve warm with heavy cream or as an accompaniment to gingerbread cake or meat dishes. *Makes approximately 3 1/2 cups*

Note: For a colorful addition, stir in a handful of cooked cranberries.

Applesauce

Apple-Mint Chutney

*Tamarind is especially used in the
cooking of India and the West Indies. Highly acidic,
tart-sweet and pasty, the tamarind adds authentic
flavor to this unique chutney.*

3 tamarind pods or 1/2 cup canned tamarind
6 tart apples (such as Greening), peeled, cored and sliced
1/2 cup raw brown sugar
1/3 cup cider vinegar
1 teaspoon chili powder
1 teaspoon salt
2 teaspoons dried mint

Soak the tamarind pods in warm water for 30
minutes. Use your fingers to squeeze the pulp from
the pods and seeds. Strain through a fine sieve.

Place the remaining ingredients, tamarind paste
and 1/3 cup water in a nonreactive kettle. Bring to
a boil, reduce the heat and simmer uncovered for 30
minutes, or until the apples are tender and mixture
is thick.

Ladle the chutney into sterilized hot pint or
half-pint canning jars, leaving approximately
1/4-inch headspace. Seal the jars with canning lids
according to manufacturer's directions and process
in a boiling water bath for 10 minutes. Cool, tighten
lids, and store. Or, cover tightly and keep in the
refrigerator up to 2 weeks. *Makes approximately
1 quart*

*Left to right: Apple-Mint Chutney,
Winter Fruit Chutney (recipe p. 48), and
Cranberry-Apple Conserve (recipe p. 46)*

Cranberry-Apple Conserve

This conserve is best served with wild game and game birds. To convert it into a sauce, just cook the mixture an additional 10 to 15 minutes and strain through a food mill. It also goes nicely with pancakes.

*4 large apples (such as Newtown Pippin
    or Jonagold), peeled, cored and sliced
1 tablespoon granulated sugar
1 cup maple syrup*

*2 cups fresh cranberries
1 tablespoon orange zest, cut into strips
    and finely diced*

Place the apples, sugar and 2 tablespoons water in a nonreactive saucepan over medium heat and steam for 5 minutes. Shake the pan to prevent the apples from sticking to the bottom. Mix in the syrup, cranberries and zest. When the berries begin to pop, reduce the heat to low, cover, stirring from time to time to prevent sticking, and cook for 10 minutes. *Makes approximately 3 cups*

Apple Butter

Truly Colonial America's first butter, it's best served on toast for grown-ups and sandwiches for kids. Depending on the sweetness of the fruit, it can be made without the addition of sugar or spices for a true fruity flavor.

*4 pounds tart apples (such as McIntosh),
    quartered with skins, pits and stems
2 cups apple cider
4 to 5 cups sugar*

*3 teaspoons ground cinnamon
2 teaspoons ground cloves
1 teaspoon ground allspice*

Combine the apples with the cider in a large, heavy-bottomed saucepan and bring to a simmer over medium heat. Simmer for 25 minutes, or until the apples are soft, stirring from time to time to prevent the apples from sticking to the bottom of the pan.

Pass the apples through a food mill placed over a large bowl. Mix in the sugar and spices and place over low heat for 4 hours, stirring often so the mixture does not scorch the pot. When the mixture is thick or when it sticks to a spoon and no rim of liquid separates around the edge, the butter is done.

Remove from the heat. Ladle into sterilized hot pint or half-pint canning jars, leaving approximately 1/4-inch headspace. Seal the jars with canning lids according to manufacturer's directions and process in a boiling water bath for 10 minutes. Cool, tighten lids, and store. Or, cover tightly and keep in the refrigerator up to 3 weeks. *Makes approximately 2 pints*

Apple-Horseradish Sauce

*Serve this piquant sauce as an accompaniment to goose, duck, smoked fish
or cold roasts such as beef and pork.*

1 tablespoon lemon juice
3 to 4 tablespoons freshly grated horseradish
3 tart apples (such as Greening), peeled and cored

1/2 cup crème fraîche (see p. 23)
Salt to taste

Place the lemon juice in a bowl. Grate the horseradish, then the apples into the juice. Stir from time to time to avoid discoloring.

Fold in the crème fraîche and season with salt. Cover and refrigerate. *Makes approximately 1 1/2 cups*

Apple Marmalade

This is a spicy version of apple butter to be used as a relish with meats and chicken.

2 pounds firm, tart apples (such as Greening)
1 tablespoon lemon juice
3 cups apple cider

3 cups sugar
1 teaspoon good quality hot curry powder

Peel, quarter and core the apples and reserve the skins and cores. Thinly slice the apples and place in a bowl of cold water and lemon juice. Set aside.

Place the skins, cores and 2 cups of water in a nonreactive saucepan and bring to a boil. Cover and simmer for 25 minutes, or until the skins are soft. Strain the liquid into a bowl, pressing down on the pulp to extract all the juices. Discard the pulp.

In a nonreactive saucepan, mix the apple liquid, cider, sugar and curry and bring to a boil and cook for 3 minutes.

Drain the apples and add to the apple liquid. Bring to a boil, reduce the heat, and simmer for 40 minutes, stirring often to prevent the apples from sticking to the bottom of the pan. When the apples are opaque, place a spoonful on a plate and set in the refrigerator. If it congeals in a few seconds, the marmalade is done.

Ladle into sterilized hot pint or half-pint canning jars, leaving approximately 1/4-inch headspace. Seal the jars with canning lids according to manufacturer's directions and process in a boiling water bath for 10 minutes. Cool, tighten lids, and store. Or, cover tightly and keep in the refrigerator up to 3 weeks. *Makes 5 cups*

Winter Fruit Chutney

In the months of October and November, farmers' markets and orchard stands offer best quality fall fruits at the best prices. This is the time to put up preserves.

4 cups firm apples (such as Golden Delicious),
    peeled, cored and cut into 1/2-inch slices
3 cups firm pears, peeled,
    cored and cut into 1/2-inch slices
1 cup quince, peeled, cored and cut into
    1/4-inch slices
Zest and juice of 2 lemons
6 cups cider vinegar
2 large onions, peeled and chopped
4 garlic cloves, peeled and minced
2 tablespoons salt

2 tablespoons mustard seed
3 tablespoons grated fresh ginger
1/2 to 1 teaspoon cayenne pepper
1 tablespoon hot pepper flakes
1 teaspoon ground cinnamon
2 cups light brown sugar, packed
1 cup granulated sugar
1 cup Sultana (golden) raisins
4 cups dark raisins
4 cups walnuts, chopped

Place the fruit in a large bowl, cover with cold water and the juice of 2 lemons. Set aside.

In a large nonreactive kettle, combine the vinegar with 2 cups cold water, lemon zest, onions, garlic, salt and spices and bring to a boil over high heat. Reduce the heat and simmer for 15 minutes, or until the onion is translucent. Add the brown and granulated sugars and fruit and bring to a boil. Lower the heat and simmer for 1 hour, stirring from time to time so the mixture does not scorch on the bottom of the pot.

When the chutney has thickened, add the raisins and nuts and cook another 15 minutes or until thick. The chutney will continue to thicken as it cools.

Ladle the chutney into sterilized hot pint or half-pint canning jars, leaving approximately 1/4-inch headspace. Seal the jars with canning lids according to manufacturer's directions and process in a boiling water bath for 10 minutes. Cool, tighten lids, and store. Or, cover tightly and keep in the refrigerator up to 3 weeks.

Allow the chutney to mellow for 3 weeks before serving. *Makes approximately 12 pints*

MAIN COURSES

Apples have found their way into endless main courses throughout the world. Possibly one of the more charming dishes I have eaten with apples was served in a little ski hut in Appenzel, home to an array of homemade local cheeses, including Ementhaler. A plate of maccaroni, tossed in butter and grated cheese and covered with fried onions and fresh chives, was served with a bowl of steaming apple compote.

Our American penchant for adding cinnamon and nutmeg to apples harks back to days when a Yankee pork dinner consisted of roasted meat dusted in cinnamon and flour and cooked in fat until golden. It was served with fried winter root vegetables and apples dusted with more spice.

In the Veneto, apples are added to the classic risotto dish, either served alone or with favored game dishes beloved by the Italians. In Germany and Alsace, apples are a natural pairing with pork and sauerkraut dishes. In Brittany and Normandy, which produces some of the finest apples in France, dishes of chicken and quail revolve around apples that are sautéed with rich butter, a reduction of cream and a splash of native Calvados—one of their finest *eau de vie* made from cider residue. The French also use cider in place of stock to imbue sauces with apple flavor.

Raclette—A Winter Party Meal

Raclette is a derivation of the French word for "scraping off."
It is now used to describe certain Swiss cheeses as well as this popular Swiss dish. When buying the cheese,
look for Swiss mountain cheeses like Aniver, Bagnes, Conches, Gosmer and Orsieres.
The rims are often embossed with the word "Raclette."

1/2 wheel Raclette
1 small jar cornichons
1 small jar sweet pickled onions
Warmed walnuts in their shells

4 or more very cold, firm apples
   (such as Winesap, Jonathan or Northern Spy)
12 to 15 hot, boiled new potatoes, in their jackets

Place a semicircle of Raclette on a board or heatproof platter. Position the board or platter at an angle next to the glowing coals of a fireplace. A brick placed underneath will do just fine.

Heat the plates until very hot and place them under the cheese as it melts. When the cheese begins to ooze freely, scrape some onto the plates, one at a time as the cheese melts.

Place the plates on underliners or wicker plate holders. Serve the cheese while bubbling with the cornichons, pickled onions, warmed walnuts, apples and potatoes.

Though not as romantic, a 500 degree F. oven will do. Bake on a heatproof platter for 10 to 15 minutes and watch carefully. Serve on very hot plates. *Serves 4 to 6*

Swiss Macaroni with Melted Gruyère and Apple Compote

This is an especially welcoming dish on a cold, snowy afternoon.

4 to 5 firm sweet apples (such as Idared or Gala),
   peeled, cored and sliced
1 teaspoon grated lemon zest
1 tablespoon granulated sugar or to taste
6 tablespoons unsalted butter
1 tablespoon vegetable oil

4 medium onions, thinly sliced
3/4 pound small elbow macaroni
8 ounces Gruyère, grated
Salt and freshly ground black pepper to taste
4 tablespoons snipped fresh chives

In a nonreactive pot, toss the apples with the lemon zest and sugar. Add 1 to 2 tablespoons of water if the apples are dry. Cover and place over a low flame and cook for approximately 10 minutes, or until the apples are soft. Shake the pan from time to time to prevent the apples from sticking. Set aside and keep warm.

In a large heavy skillet, melt 3 tablespoons of butter with the vegetable oil over medium high heat. Add the onions and sauté until crisp and golden brown.

While the onions are cooking, prepare the macaroni according to package directions.

Drain the macaroni and toss with the remaining 3 tablespoons butter and cheese and salt and pepper to taste.

Divide the macaroni among 4 warm plates. Top each plate of macaroni with the onions and generously sprinkle the chives on top. Serve with the apple compote on the side.
Serves 4

Risotto with Apples

The Golden Delicious is the best apple to use for this risotto.
It remains hard for the first 10 minutes of cooking, then, when you least
expect it, it puffs and explodes, becoming soft and tender.

1 cup Golden Delicious apples (approximately
    1 large apple), peeled, cored and diced
4 to 5 cups chicken stock,
    homemade or low-sodium canned
2 tablespoons unsalted butter
2 tablespoons olive oil

1 small onion, peeled and minced
2 cups Arborio rice
1/2 cup dry white wine
1/3 cup grated Parmesan cheese plus extra
    for serving
3 or 4 gratings fresh nutmeg

Place the apples in a small saucepan, cover and cook over medium heat until soft, approximately 10 minutes. Shake the pan from time to time so that the apples do not stick. Set aside.

In a saucepan, bring the stock to a simmer and continue to keep hot over low heat.

In a medium nonreactive saucepan, heat the butter and oil over medium heat. When the butter mixture begins to foam, add the onion and sauté until translucent, approximately 5 minutes.

Add the rice and cook, stirring constantly with a wooden spoon. When the rice has absorbed most of the butter, add the wine and cook, stirring constantly until the rice has absorbed the wine.

Continue to stir and add the stock 1 ladle at a time. When the rice has been cooking for 10 minutes, add the cooked apples. Continue adding the stock until the rice is cooked but slightly chewy, approximately 15 minutes. You may not need all the stock.

Fold in the Parmesan cheese and the nutmeg and cook for another minute or so.

Divide the risotto among 4 warm plates and serve immediately with extra grated Parmesan cheese. *Serves 4*

Chicken Curry

*It was the British Colonialists who brought curry back from India. They paired it with apples when
making curry dishes and added it to chutneys made with apples to accompany the dish.*

2 tablespoons peanut or vegetable oil
One 3 1/2-pound chicken, backbone and
    wing tips removed and cut into 8 pieces
    with skin and bone intact; reserve the backbone
    and wings for stock
3 tablespoons unsalted butter
3 medium onions, chopped
3 garlic cloves, chopped
2 hot green chili peppers (jalapeños),
    seeded, ribs removed and cut into 1/8-inch dice
1-inch piece fresh ginger, grated
2 tart apples (such as Newtown Pippin or Green-
    ing), peeled, cored and cut into 1/4-inch dice

2 tablespoons good quality curry powder
2 tablespoons fresh
    or unsweetened canned shredded coconut meat
2 cardamom seeds, crushed
1/3 cup plain yogurt
1 3/4 cups chicken stock,
    homemade or low-sodium canned
1 stalk lemon grass, peeled
    or 2-inch piece of lemon zest
Salt to taste
1 tablespoon lemon juice
2 tablespoons chopped fresh cilantro

In a large nonreactive skillet, heat the oil over high heat. Brown the chicken pieces on all sides and set aside.

Pour off the fat from the pan and add the butter. When the butter begins to foam, add the onions and garlic and sauté until translucent, approximately 5 minutes. Add the chilies, ginger and apples and cook another 3 minutes, or until the apples begin to soften. Mix in the curry powder and cook a minute or so until blended. Add the coconut, cardamom and yogurt and mix thoroughly. Add the chicken pieces and cook a minute or so until all the ingredients are blended.

Add the stock and lemon grass and season with salt. Bring to a boil, reduce the heat and simmer for 1 hour, stirring from time to time. Stir in the lemon juice and cilantro.

Remove the lemon grass and serve with boiled rice. *Serves 4*

Boudin with Sautéed Apples

In France, boudin is always served with sautéed or fried apples. This version is lighter.

1/2 cup dried apples, diced
1/4 cup applejack or Calvados
1/2 pound rabbit meat or chicken breast, skinned
    and boned
1/2 pound lean pork, trimmed of all fat
1/3 pound pork fat
1 cup heavy cream
1 tablespoon chopped fresh parsley
1/4 teaspoon chopped fresh sage leaves
1/4 teaspoon chopped fresh thyme

1 teaspoon cayenne pepper
1/8 teaspoon ground cumin
Pinch of allspice
1 teaspoon salt
4 tablespoons (1/2 stick) unsalted butter
1 small onion, finely chopped
2 egg yolks
12 natural casings for stuffing sausages
4 Golden Delicious apples, to accompany the boudin

Prepare the boudin mixture: In a small bowl, soak the dried apples with the applejack and enough water to cover and set aside until they are plump.

Cut the meats and pork fat into small cubes. Combine the meats and fat and grind in an electric grinder. Pass the mixture through the grinder a second time. Place the mixture in a large bowl and set aside.

Place the cream in a heavy saucepan over medium heat and reduce by half. Let cool.

Drain the apples. Add the apples, herbs and seasonings to the meat mixture and mix well.

In a medium skillet, melt 2 tablespoons of butter over medium heat and sauté the onions until they are translucent, approximately 5 minutes.

Whisk the egg yolks with the cream and add to the meat mixture. Add the onions and combine.

Melt the remaining butter in the skillet over medium heat. Add the boudin mixture and cook for approximately 7 minutes, stirring constantly. Cool the mixture.

When cool, stuff the boudin mixture into natural casings using an electric sausage stuffer. Chill until ready to use. Mixture should make approximately 12 small boudins.

Grill the boudins under a hot broiler or sauté them in a lightly buttered nonstick pan for approximately 10 to 12 minutes.

While the sausage is cooking, peel and core the apples and cut them into eighths.

Arrange the apples in a nonstick pan and place over medium heat. Cook the apples until they are tender and golden on each side. Serve with the boudin. *Serves 4*

Sautéed Quail with Cream and Calvados

As sophisticated as this dish may sound,
it is typical of the regional food served from Brittany to Normandy,
where apples, Calvados and cream abound.

4 quail, split, backbone and wing tips removed
Salt and freshly ground black pepper
Flour for dusting
8 tablespoons (1 stick) unsalted butter
1 tablespoon canola oil

3 firm, sweet apples (such as Golden Delicious
  or Greening), peeled, quartered and cored
1 tablespoon granulated sugar
1 cup heavy cream
1 ounce Calvados

Preheat the oven to 325 degrees F.

Reserve or freeze the backbone and wing tips for a game stock.

Wash the quail and pat dry with paper towels. Season with salt and pepper and lightly dust with flour.

In a large heavy skillet, add 4 tablespoons butter and the oil over medium high heat. When the butter is foamy, place the quail in the skillet, skin side down. Place a flat plate and weight over the quail and cook for 5 minutes, or until golden. Turn the quail and repeat with the weight for another 5 minutes.

Place the quail skin side up in an oven-proof pan and place in the oven.

Slice each apple quarter into thirds. Drain the fat from the skillet and return to medium heat. Melt the remaining butter and add the apples. Sprinkle with salt and sugar and brown the apples on both sides. Add the cream and Calvados and bring to a boil. Reduce the heat and simmer for approximately 7 minutes, or until the apples are soft but still holding their shape.

With a slotted spoon, divide the apples between 2 warm plates. Bring the sauce to a boil. Place 2 quail on each plate and stir pan juices into the cream mixture. Cook the sauce for another minute or so and strain the sauce over the quail. *Serves 2*

Roast Pork Loin with Glazed Vegetables, Prunes and Apples

Homegrown pigs dine on apples before trundling off to pig heaven.
Though commercially raised pigs may not have been treated as well, cooking pork
with apples, dried fruits or cider makes up for the oversight.

One 5-pound pork loin, boned, rolled and tied
2 tablespoons chopped fresh sage leaves
Salt and freshly ground black pepper
2 cups dry apple cider
12 dried prunes
1 lemon slice
6 small turnips, peeled, cut into olive shapes,
    approximately 12 pieces
12 small onions, blanched and peeled

6 carrots, peeled and cut into 1/4-inch rounds
Granulated sugar
6 large firm tart apples
    (such as Northern Spy or Granny Smith),
    peeled, cored, halved and cut into thirds
1 tablespoon Dijon-style mustard
1/2 cup crème fraîche (see p. 23)
    or 2/3 cup heavy cream reduced by half

Preheat the oven to 325 degrees F.

Rub the pork loin with the sage and season with salt and pepper. Place the loin on a rack in a roasting pan, pour in 1 cup of cider and roast for 1 hour. Baste from time to time.

Place the prunes and lemon slice in a small bowl, cover with boiling water and set aside.

After an hour of cooking the loin, remove 1/2 cup of pan juices from the roasting pan. In a bowl, toss the turnips, onions and carrots separately with the pan juices and dust with a little sugar. Sprinkle the vegetables around the bottom of the roasting pan with any remaining juice. Cook for another half hour.

Remove another 1/2 cup of pan juices and toss with the apples, sprinkle with sugar and return to the roasting pan. Continue cooking until the roast is cooked, approximately 1 1/2 hours or 20 minutes per pound. Turn the vegetables and apples from time to time to brown evenly.

Drain the prunes and remove any pits. Reserve the prunes and their liquid.

Place the roast, apples and vegetables on a warm platter, cover with foil and keep warm.

Remove most of the fat from the roasting pan. Set the pan over high heat and add the remaining cup of cider and 1/2 cup of prune liquid. Bring to a boil scraping up the brown bits. Mix in the mustard and season with salt and pepper and continue to cook until the sauce begins to glaze and thicken.

Strain the sauce into a saucepan and add the prunes. Bring to a boil, reduce the heat and simmer a couple of minutes until the prunes are hot. Remove the prunes with a slotted spoon and arrange on the platter with the roast and vegetables.

Whisk the crème fraîche into the sauce and heat for a minute or so and pour into a warm sauce boat. Serve with the roast. *Serves 6*

SWEETS

James Beard once asked me if I had ever eaten mock apple pie—that recipe which appeared on the box of Ritz crackers. I said I hadn't. He looked away and confessed, "It isn't so bad if you're hungry. But I prefer the real McCoy." And so do I.

During our early Colonial era, when the brick oven was turning out baked bean dishes, hoe cakes, bannocks and puddings, the apple pandowdy, Yankee Apple John and Apple Betty were cooking alongside. At the end of supper, the warm oven was swept clean and a pie, cobbler or crisp was cooked as the oven cooled and served at breakfast. The earthen dish was filled with sliced apples, sweetened with maple sugar or syrup, bits of diced pork, cinnamon and nutmeg, and covered with a crust. These ingredients are still our basic inspiration. For those who are not fond of cinnamon, cloves or nutmeg, substituting grated lemon zest will bring out the true flavor and perfume of the apple. Although margarine, oil and butter have replaced the pork lard, I join in with all those mid-Western apple pie contestants who claim that the flakiest crust for an apple pie is made with lard.

Caramel Apples

These gooey delights are an easy dessert for kids to make. McIntosh are the only apples to use.

4 to 5 McIntosh apples
1 cup granulated sugar
3/4 cup dark corn syrup

1 cup heavy cream
2 tablespoons unsalted butter
1 teaspoon vanilla extract

Wash and dry the apples, remove the stems and stick a wooden skewer into each stem end. Set skewered apples aside.

In a small saucepan, combine the sugar, syrup, cream and butter and place over high heat. Bring to a boil for 3 to 5 minutes, or until it registers 245 degrees F. on a candy thermometer.

Remove from the heat and swirl in the vanilla. Quickly dip the apples, one at a time, into the caramel and spoon over the apples to cover completely. Hold the skewer between the palms of your hands and spin for a moment to cool. Place upright on waxed paper. *Makes 4 to 5 candied apples*

Caramelized Baked Apples

*Sugar and spice aren't necessary when baking just-picked apples. A little cider in the pan is all you need,
and when there is none, I throw in the peels and core with a cup of water to intensify the flavor.*

6 medium apples (such as Romes or Cortlands)
3/4 cup apple cider

Caramel:
1/3 cup corn syrup
1 cup granulated sugar

Crème Anglaise:
2 cups milk
1 cup heavy cream
1/2 vanilla bean, split or 1 teaspoon vanilla extract
4 egg yolks
1/2 cup sugar

Preheat the oven to 375 degrees F.

Core the apples and peel the skin away, leaving approximately a 1 1/2-inch band around the apples.

Place the apples in an ovenproof baking dish approximately 2 inches apart and pour the cider over the apples. Bake for 40 minutes, or until the apples are soft but not mushy. Using a bulb baster, baste the apples once or twice.

Arrange on serving plates and discard the juice. Cool the apples before coating with caramel.

In a bowl, combine the syrup with 1/3 cup boiling water and set aside. In a saucepan add the sugar and combine with the syrup mixture over high heat by swirling the pan. Remove from the heat and continue to swirl until the sugar is dissolved. Do not use a spoon.

Return to the heat and bring to a boil. Continue to swirl the pan until the syrup is golden. Remove from the heat and quickly spoon the caramel over the apples.

Prepare the crème anglaise: Over high heat, in a heavy-bottomed saucepan, bring the milk and cream to a boil. If using a vanilla bean, add it to the milk to infuse with flavor. Remove from the heat and let sit for 10-15 minutes.

In a medium bowl, beat the yolks and sugar together until thick and lemon-colored. Add the hot milk and cream.

Return the mixture to the pan and cook over low heat or in a double broiler, stirring constantly until mixture thickens and coats the back of a spoon (approximately 10 minutes). Remove the custard from heat and strain through a fine sieve into a clean bowl over ice. If using vanilla extract, add in at this point. Use custard immediately or refrigerate with plastic wrap up to 24 hours. *Makes 2 cups of crème anglaise*

Serve the caramelized apples with whipped cream or crème anglaise. *Serves 6*

Apple and Dried Cranberry Crisp

The piquant cranberries give a little zing to this sweet and easy dessert created by Jon Gilman.

Topping:
1/2 cup pecan halves
1 cup all-purpose flour
1/3 cup light brown sugar
4 tablespoons granulated sugar
1/8 teaspoon cinnamon
1 tablespoon grated orange zest
1/3 cup unsalted butter, softened

Filling:
6 apples (such as Golden Delicious or Idared),
approximately 2 pounds, peeled, cored and sliced
1 tablespoon granulated sugar, or to taste
1/2 cup dried cranberries

Preheat the oven to 350 degrees F. Toast the pecans for 5 minutes. Cool and chop.

In a large bowl, combine the dry ingredients and zest and work the softened butter in with your fingers. When the mixture resembles coarse sand, add the pecans and set aside.

Raise the oven temperature to 375 degrees F. In a bowl, sprinkle the apples with a little sugar and mix with the dried cranberries. Place the filling into a baking dish, level, and spoon the topping evenly over the apples.

Cover with foil and bake for 20 minutes. Remove the foil and continue baking for 20 minutes, or until the top is crisp and browned and apples are tender. Serve with ice cream or crème anglaise (see p. 72). *Serves 6 to 8*

Apple Brown Betty

Brown Betty is everyone's favorite and as Yankee as you can get. Sherry makes the difference.

12 tablespoons (1 1/2 sticks) unsalted butter
Approximately 3 cups fresh bread crumbs
6 firm apples (such as Cortland, Winesap, Northern
Spy), peeled, cored and sliced very thin
10 ounces red currant jelly
2 ounces dry sherry
Whipped cream for serving (optional)

Preheat the oven to 375 degrees F.

Generously butter a 5-cup loaf pan. Dust the bottom of the pan with 1/8-inch thickness of bread crumbs. Cover the bread crumbs with bits of shaved butter. Top with a layer of apples slightly overlaping. Spread a thin layer of currant jelly over the apples. Repeat the layering again. When you have reached the third layer of apples, press the apples down and continue to fill the pan in this order, pressing down on each apple layer before continuing. You should have 5 layers of apples when you reach the top. End with a dusting of bread crumbs and the remaining butter.

Cover with foil and bake 15 minutes. Remove the foil and continue to bake for 40 minutes (30 minutes if using a soft apple). Sprinkle the sherry over the top and bake another 5 minutes, or until the top is golden and the apples can be pierced easily with a sharp knife. Cool and serve warm with whipped cream. *Serves 6*

All-Purpose Pie Crust

*This all-purpose crust works well for
most pies, tarts and turnovers.*

3 cups all-purpose flour, sifted
1 teaspoon salt
1 cup (8 ounces) lard,
    margarine or unsalted butter, cut into bits
1 egg
1/3 cup milk

Sift the flour and salt into the bowl of an electric mixer. Add the lard and mix with a pastry paddle at low speed until the mixture is the consistency of fine cornmeal.

In a medium bowl, whisk the egg and milk and pour into the flour mixture. Increase the speed and mix until the dough forms a ball and pulls away from the sides of the bowl. Divide the dough into 3 equal pieces and wrap in plastic wrap and refrigerate 2 of the balls for at least 20 minutes. Freeze the third ball for another use.

On a heavily floured surface, roll out 1 ball into a 1/8-inch thick circle large enough to fill and slightly overlap the edge of a 9- to 10-inch pie pan. Transfer the crust to the ungreased pan and trim the excess dough and press down the edges. Brush the pie shell with the melted butter and set aside. *Makes enough pastry for 1 double crusted pie plus a bottom or top crust for a second*

American Apple Pie

*The best apple pie crusts are made with lard.
Margarine is a health-conscious substitute.*

1 pie crust

Filling:
8 cups sweet-tart firm apples
    (such as 4 Northern Spies or 6 Idareds),
    peeled, cored and sliced
1 tablespoon granulated sugar
2 tablespoons all-purpose flour
1 teaspoon vanilla
1/2 cup half-and-half

Preheat the oven to 425 degrees F.

In a large bowl, toss the apples with the sugar and flour and combine with vanilla and half-and-half. Set aside.

Moisten the edges of a bottom pie crust with a little water and fill the crust-lined pan with the apple filling. Place the top crust over the apples. Seal and crimp the edges. Cut approximately 8 small vents in the top crust by inserting a pairing knife into the dough. For a more elaborate presentation, cover with a lattice crust.

Bake for 10 minutes and reduce the temperature to 350 and bake 30 to 40 minutes, or until the crust is golden and the apples are tender when pierced with a trussing needle.

Cool and serve with vanilla ice cream, crème anglaise (see p. 72) or sliced sharp Cheddar cheese. *Serves 8 to 10*

Apple Tart

*The big free-formed tart is a rustic
dessert served in the fall at the home of friends
of mine in the hills of Provence.*

1 recipe pie dough made with butter
    plus 1 tablespoon granulated sugar
    sifted with the flour (see p. 76)
4 or 5 apples (such as Golden Delicious),
    peeled, cored and sliced 1/4 inch thick
1 tablespoon lemon juice
3 tablespoons granulated sugar
1/3 cup apricot jam

Preheat the oven to 425 degrees F.

Toss the sliced apples with the lemon juice
and set aside.

On a lightly floured surface, roll out 2/3 of
the pie dough into a long rectangle, approximately 1/8-inch thick, to fit a large flat baking
sheet. Place the pastry on the sheet. Reserve or
freeze the remaining pie dough for another use.

Cover the pastry with the apples in rows,
overlapping slightly and leaving an inch of
pastry around the rectangle. Fold the rim of the
pastry up to, and slightly overlapping, the
apples. Dust apples with 2 tablespoons sugar.

Bake for 25 to 30 minutes, or until the
apples and crust are browned. Remove from
the oven and dust with the remaining tablespoon sugar.

Melt the apricot jam over medium heat.
Using a pastry brush, lightly glaze the apples
with the brush. *Serves 8 to 10*

Apple Sorbet

*Apple sorbet is a refreshing entremet
at any grand dinner and an especially festive
dessert when served with sauce anglaise or
warm caramel sauce.*

6 red apples (such as Idared, Cortland or Rome)
1 tablespoon lemon juice
4 cups water
3/4 cup granulated sugar, or to taste
1 teaspoon vanilla extract

Wash the apples and cut them into quarters
with their skin and seeds. Place the apples in a
nonreactive saucepan and mix with the lemon
juice. Add the water and sugar and bring to a
boil over high heat.

Reduce the heat, cover and simmer for 45
minutes, or until the apples are soft and mushy.
Stir in the vanilla.

Strain the mixture into a bowl through a
food mill and discard the skin and pits. Refrigerate until cold.

Pour the mixture into an ice cream machine and freeze according to the manufacturer's
directions. *Makes approximately 1 quart*

Apple Turnovers

*Turnovers were a winter breakfast treat made with
the extra pie dough my mother saved from her apple pies.*

1 recipe pie dough, made with
    margarine or unsalted butter (see p. 76)

Filling:
1/2 pound (approximately 1 cup) dried cherries
1/2 cup apple cider
1 cup walnuts, chopped
1/4 cup granulated sugar

1/2 teaspoon ground cinnamon
A few gratings of fresh nutmeg
1 teaspoon grated orange zest
1 tablespoon unsalted butter
4 medium firm apples (such as Rome),
    peeled, cored and thinly sliced
1 egg
Granulated sugar for dusting

In a bowl, soak the cherries, cider and 1/3 cup boiling water for 1 hour or until they plump up.

In a medium saucepan, combine the cherries and juice, walnuts, sugar, cinnamon, nutmeg and orange zest. Cook over medium heat for 5 minutes, or until the cherries have absorbed most of the liquid, stirring often to prevent scorching on the bottom of the pan. Set aside and reserve.

Melt the butter in a medium nonstick skillet over medium heat. Add the apples and sauté until apples are tender but still retain their shape.

In a large bowl, combine the apples with the cherry mixture and cool.

Cut the pastry in half. On a lightly floured surface, roll out one half in a large square approximately 1/8-inch thick. Using a 4- to 4 1/2-inch diameter cookie cutter, cut the pastry into 8 squares, dipping the cutter in flour to prevent sticking. Place approximately 1 heaping tablespoon of the filling on each square of dough.

In a small bowl, beat the egg with 1 tablespoon cold water and brush the egg wash around the edges. Fold over into a triangle and gently crimp the edges.

Line a baking sheet with parchment and place the turnovers on the sheet. Refrigerate for 20 minutes.

Repeat with the remaining half of the dough and filling.

Preheat the oven to 350 degrees F.

Trim the edges of each turnover with a serrated pastry cutter. Brush the tops with the remaining egg wash and make 2 or 3 slits on top with a pairing knife. Sprinkle lightly with sugar.

Bake for 30 to 35 minutes or until the turnovers are golden and lightly browned.

Cool on a pastry rack. *Makes approximately 16 turnovers*

Apple Pancake

*This pancake harks back to days at my grandmother's
when she would whip up a couple, all golden and fluffy, and serve them after
a pot roast dinner. Serve as a late breakfast or with afternoon tea.*

Batter:
1/2 cup all-purpose flour
1 tablespoon granulated sugar
1/2 teaspoon baking powder
Pinch of salt
4 eggs
1 cup milk
2 tablespoons unsalted butter, melted
2 teaspoons grated orange zest
1 teaspoon vanilla extract
Generous grating of nutmeg

Fruit Mixture:
4 tablespoons (1/2 stick) unsalted butter
1/2 cup granulated sugar
1/2 teaspoon cinnamon
1/8 teaspoon freshly grated nutmeg
2 large tart apples (such as Greening),
*   peeled, halved, cored and thinly sliced*
Confectioners' sugar for dusting (optional)

In a large bowl, sift the flour, sugar, baking powder and salt. In a medium bowl, whisk the eggs and add the milk, beating until smooth. Fold the flour into the egg mixture and add the melted butter, zest, vanilla and nutmeg. Beat until smooth. Set aside for 30 minutes.

Preheat the oven to 425 degrees F.

Prepare the fruit mixture: Melt the butter in a 10-inch ovenproof skillet over medium heat. Rotate the pan and coat the sides with the butter and remove from the heat.

Combine sugar and spices and sprinkle half the mixture into the skillet. Layer the apple slices evenly over the pan and sprinkle the remaining sugar mixture over the apples.

Place the skillet over medium high heat. When the sugar begins to bubble, pour the batter evenly over the apples. Place the skillet in the oven and bake for 10 minutes. Reduce heat to 375 degrees F. and bake an additional 10 minutes, or until the pancake is golden and the center a little soft.

Pull the pancake away from the sides of the pan with a spatula and slide onto a heated serving platter. Dust with confectioners' sugar.
Serves 4

Apple Snow

This mousselike dessert is a refreshing end to a rich meal.

3 1/2 cups applesauce (see p. 42) (see p. 42)
2 egg whites

1/8 teaspoon lemon juice
1/3 cup granulated sugar

Chill the applesauce. In the bowl of an electric mixer, beat the whites with the lemon juice at low speed. When the whites are frothy, gradually add the sugar, beating until the whites form a stiff and glossy meringue. Fold the meringue into the chilled applesauce and refrigerate until chilled. *Serves 4*

BEVERAGES

In our history, 19th century America was a very hospitable time and it was not unusual for the merest stranger to be offered a libation of one sort or other. It was commonplace for a traveler, just passing down some country road, to be invited in by a kindly farmer's wife and be offered a refreshing drink. More often than not, he would also join the family for supper. One of the simplest and cheapest drinks always on hand was appleaid—a quart of boiling water poured over two sliced apples with a little sugar. When it was cool, the liquid was strained and sweetened and drunk cold or with ice.

A child's thirst was quenched with sweet, unfermented cider, but a man's, slaked with hard cider or apple brandy. Our immigrant forefathers missed their clarets, but home-brewed apple beverages kept many an English and Dutch Colonist happy. Apple cider was drunk straight, served hot with rum, fermented into sparkling cider with a little kick, and distilled into a liquor called applejack. Though not as sophisticated as Calvados, its French counterpart, applejack has a punch all its own. Today, we still enjoy many of the popular apple drink recipes handed down to us over time.

Apple Brandy Cocktail

*This sophisticated cocktail appears at bars
where a good barman works his art.*

1 1/2 ounces apple brandy
1 teaspoon grenadine syrup
1 teaspoon lemon juice

Fill a cocktail shaker with ice and add all the
ingredients. Shake until the shaker frosts and
strain into a chilled glass. *Makes 1 cocktail*

Hot Rum and Cider

A festive drink on cold winter evenings.

2 tablespoons unsalted butter, at room temperature
1 1/2 tablespoons maple sugar
4 long strips of orange zest
8 cloves
4 cinnamon sticks
4 ounces dark rum
2 1/2 cups hot apple cider

Cream the butter with the sugar and set aside.
Stud 2 cloves in each strip of orange. In
each glass or mug, place the zest, cinnamon
stick and an ounce of rum. Pour in 4 to 5
ounces of hot cider and top with a little butter
mixture. *Makes 4 drinks*

Hot Rum and Cider

Left to right: Cape Cod Jack, Apple Cocktail, Apple Blossom and Sparkling Cider Punch

Cape Cod Jack

*Cranberry juice mixed with liquors
may have sprung from New England,
but its popularity is everywhere.*

*2 ounces applejack
2 ounces cranberry juice
1 tablespoon granulated sugar syrup*

Fill a large old fashion glass with ice, add all the ingredients, and stir. *Makes 1 drink*

Apple Cocktail

*Applejack is a legacy from the Colonists—
their substitute for brandy. Added to a combination
of liquors, it has real punch.*

*1 ounce applejack
1 ounce apple cider
1/2 ounce gin
1/2 ounce Cognac*

Pour all the ingredients over ice in a cocktail shaker. Shake until the shaker frosts and pour into chilled cocktail glasses. *Makes 2 cocktails*

Apple Blossom

*The rough edge of Calvados is smoothed with
the addition of velvety vermouth.*

*1 ounce Calvados or applejack
1 ounce Italian sweet vermouth
1/2 ounce light rum
1/2 teaspoon Grenadine
1 teaspoon lemon juice*

Fill a cocktail shaker with ice and add all the ingredients. Shake until the shaker frosts and strain into a chilled cocktail glass. *Makes 1 cocktail*

Sparkling Cider Punch

*Try this bubbling variation without the
expense of buying Champagne.*

*1 teaspoon superfine sugar
1/2 teaspoon lemon juice
1 ounce applejack
Sparkling apple cider, chilled*

Combine the sugar, lemon juice and applejack in a tall highball glass. Stir a few moments until the sugar dissolves. Add 3 ice cubes and fill with sparkling cider. *Makes 1 drink*

INDEX

ACKNOWLEDGEMENTS

I would like to thank all those friends and colleagues who helped and cheered this little book on: Ted Donahue, a fast and furious researcher, Jon Gilman, Clay and Nevin who voted on the best apple pie, and Cheryl Merser for all her good help. Special thanks to all those at Collins Publishing, San Francisco, especially Lena Tabori for including me in this series, Jenny Barry for her design and art direction, Meesha Halm for her editing, Kathryn Kleinman for her beautiful photography and Stephanie Greenleigh for her food styling.

—Christopher Idone

Photography Acknowledgements:

Collins and the photography team would also like to thank the following: Michaele Thunen, floral and prop stylist; Michele Miller and Dimitri Spathis, photo assistants; Pat Brill, food stylist's assistant; Barbara Beal, Jim and Rosemary Jolley and Penelope Hunt, location; Mimi Luebbermann and Sara Slavin, props; Harmony Farm Supplies; Davies and Starr; Bonnie Grossman at AMES Gallery in Berkeley; Cyclamen Pottery in Berkeley; Bill Fujimoto from Monterey Market, Berkeley, CA; The International Apple Institute; and the Washington State Apple Commission.

Approximate Metric Conversions

Liquid Weights

U.S. Measurements	Metric Equivalents
1/4 teaspoon	1.23 ml
1/2 teaspoon	2.5 ml
3/4 teaspoon	3.7 ml
1 teaspoon	5 ml
1 dessertspoon	10 ml
1 tablespoon (3 teaspoons)	15 ml
2 tablespoons (1 ounce)	30 ml
1/4 cup	60 ml
1/3 cup	80 ml
1/2 cup	120 ml
2/3 cup	160 ml
3/4 cup	180 ml
1 cup (8 ounces)	240 ml
2 cups (1 pint)	480 ml
3 cups	720 ml
4 cups (1 quart)	1 litre
4 quarts (1 gallon)	3 3/4 litres

Dry Weights

U.S. Measurements	Metric Equivalents
1/4 ounce	7 grams
1/3 ounce	10 grams
1/2 ounce	14 grams
1 ounce	28 grams
1 1/2 ounces	42 grams
1 3/4 ounces	50 grams
2 ounces	57 grams
3 ounces	85 grams
3 1/2 ounces	100 grams
4 ounces (1/4 pound)	114 grams
6 ounces	170 grams
8 ounces (1/2 pound)	227 grams
9 ounces	250 grams
16 ounces (1 pound)	464 grams

Temperatures

Farenheit	Celsius (Centigrade)
32°F (water freezes)	0°C
200°F	95°C
212°F (water boils)	100°C
250°F	120°C
275°F	135°C
300°F (slow oven)	150°C
325°F	160°C
350°F (moderate oven)	175°C
375°F	190°C
400°F (hot oven)	205°C
425°F	220°C
450°F (very hot oven)	230°C
475°F	245°C
500°F (extremely hot oven)	260°C

Length

U.S. Measurements	Metric Equivalents
1/8 inch	3 mm
1/4 inch	6 mm
3/8 inch	1 cm
1/2 inch	1.2 cm
1 inch	2.5 cm
3/4 inch	2 cm
1 1/4 inches	3.1 cm
1 1/2 inches	3.7 cm
2 inches	5 cm
3 inches	7.5 cm
4 inches	10 cm
5 inches	12.5 cm

Approximate Equivalents

1 kilo is slightly more than 2 pounds
1 litre is slightly more than 1 quart
1 meter is slightly over 3 feet
1 centimeter is approximately 3/8 inch